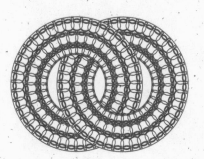

LIMITED EDITIONS

LIMITED
EDITIONS

CAROLE STONE

CAVANKERRY
PRESS

CavanKerry Press Ltd.
Fort Lee, New Jersey
www.cavankerrypress.org

Publisher's Cataloging-in-Publication Data
provided by Five Rainbows Cataloging Services
Names: Stone, Carole, 1930- author.
Title: Limited editions / Carole Stone.
Description: Fort Lee, NJ : CavanKerry Press, 2023.
Identifiers: ISBN 978-1-960327-00-0 (paperback)
Subjects: LCSH: Grief—Poetry. | Marriage—Poetry. | Widows—Poetry. | Terminal care—Poetry. | Poetry. | Women authors. | BISAC: POETRY / Subjects & Themes / Death, Grief, Loss. | POETRY / Subjects & Themes / Family. | POETRY / Women Authors.
Classification: LCC PS3569.T6297 A6 2023 (print) | LCC PS3569.T6297 (ebook) | DDC 811/.54—dc23.

Cover artwork: Kitchen Still Life with Fish and Cat (circa 1650), Circle of Sebastian Stoskopff (German, 1597–1657)
Cover and interior text design by Mayfly Design
First Edition 2023, Printed in the United States of America

CAVANKERRY
PRESS

 Made possible by funds from the
New Jersey State Council on the Arts, a partner
agency of the National Endowment for the Arts.

CavanKerry Press is grateful for the support it receives
from the New Jersey State Council on the Arts, the
National Endowment for the Arts, and the New Jersey
Arts and Culture Renewal Fund.

In addition, CavanKerry Press gratefully acknowledges
generous grants and emergency support received during
the COVID-19 pandemic from the following funders:

The Academy of American Poets

Community of Literary Magazines and Presses

National Book Foundation

New Jersey Council for the Humanities

New Jersey Economic Development Authority

Northern New Jersey Community Foundation

The Poetry Foundation

US Small Business Administration

Also by Carole Stone

Legacy (1979)

A Sentimental Education (1981)

Giving Each Other Up (1985)

Orphan in the Movie House (1997)

Lime and Salt (1997)

More Sweet, More Salt (2005)

Traveling with the Dead (2007)

Paris Etudes (2008)

American Rhapsody (2012)

Hurt, the Shadow (2013)

Late (2016)

All We Have Is Our Voice (2018)

For Harold

*Two by two in the ark of
the ache of it.*

—Denise Levertov

CONTENTS

III

IV

V

Fortune

Dear dying
and dead,

forgive me
my daily wants.

I split open
a fortune cookie.

Its paper words
are in my mouth.

Small print,
ideograms

to decipher.
I bite down hard.

I

Blind Date

We met on a blind date.
"He's cute," the woman from your hometown,
Woonsocket, who introduced us, said.
And you were, standing by the front door
in khakis and a button-down shirt.

We drove to Rolf's Restaurant in Irvington,
sat at the bar. You didn't say a word.
Enough of being the vivacious one
on blind dates, I told myself.
This one better talk.

And you did, explaining
the scene in the pub in *Ulysses*
where The Citizen asks Bloom
"What is your nation?" And that's when I knew
you would be mine.

Joyce Group

We look out the window at a cold cloudy sky,
decide we're not too tired to take the 66 to Manhattan.

You carry the hardback copy of *Ulysses* for me.
The snowstorm turned the city streets gray as an elephant.

A dog walker pulls three poodles. In Bleecker Street Playground,
like lifers, old men bend over chessboards.

In the middle of Eighth a man dodges traffic,
yelling, "Hey, it's good, all good."

The Korean grocer displays chrysanthemums,
pink as the December sunset.

We buy a bouquet to give to the group's host.
I ask you what we'll do

when we finish Joyce's books.
You laugh. "Read them again!"

Grounded

My wedding dress was a three-quarter sleeve
green knee-length taffeta,
crinoline stiff as a washboard.

Irma, my high school best friend,
sent champagne. Aunt Elsie sat
like a distant relative

on the sofa my parents left me,
Uncle Sid beside her,
his three chins sunk into his chest.

I clutched your hand;
the judge pronounced us man and wife.
Grandmother wept. "So pretty," she sobbed.

Outside, a February blizzard,
planes grounded
for our Acapulco honeymoon.

We slept at the airport.
The beginning of the ups and downs
of forever.

Day Trip to Brighton

Brighton's pier—
jellied eels, candied apples,

babies in strollers, fair-skinned
English mums turn pink.

Teatime.
Bits of sugar between our teeth,

we sipped small kindnesses
from blue china cups.

Sometimes you were me.
Sometimes I was you.

By the beautiful sea,
on green-striped deck chairs,

husband and wife, wordless
in the sun we nodded off.

The Luxembourg Gardens

On a hot Sunday afternoon,
cranky and tired
from the Metro crowds, we stepped
into the Luxembourg Gardens,
past a statue of an embracing couple,
limbs frozen in desire.

In the gazebo a brass band
played *The Radetzky March*,
the string section out of tune.
We didn't care and applauded
when the leader bowed.

We rested on a bench,
my head on your lap
as if we were just beginning
our lives together, young
and ignorant of what lay ahead.
Even the pigeons that splattered us
couldn't change this moment.

We walked away from the Medici Fountain,
the two chestnut trees that bent over us
like a mother and father
happy their children found pleasure.

Long Marriage

You are planting snap peas.
Knees in dirt, you pat the earth, the way you rubbed
our daughter's back when she cried.

You rest against the stockade fence,
half-smiling, half-frowning, talking a little to yourself.
I hear your huge sighs, which you deny.

You come inside for your plaid gabardine jacket.
I'm in our kitchen, still married
after forty years to a man who finishes

The Times crossword each morning.
I chop onions; you read Szymborska's *Collected Poems*
that I checked out of the library.

You close the book, pull on your garden gloves.
I want to know why peas need a fence to lean on.
"That's the way it is," you say.

In the Matter of Pumpkin Soup

"No one likes Dad's soup,"
my daughter tells me.
"It's cold, too spicy."

She's a mother now,
the child who sat cross-legged,
round and good as a Winesap

on the nursery school floor.
Each Thanksgiving,
her father chooses a fat pumpkin,

scoops out the seeds,
boils and mashes the yellow rind,
mixes in the heavy cream.

I can't make this man change.
I tell my daughter—
eat.

Farmers' Market

Saturdays we drive
to the Farmers' Market,
pull into a handicap space.

We buy corn, tomatoes, apples
where the overfriendly
server helps fill our shopping bags,

asks, "Did you find your wallet
from last week?"
"In my other purse," I reply.

"I hope I'm not losing my grip."
"All of us are," she says.
With multiple trips to our car,

a bag or two at a time,
we find comfort among the stalls
of nut-raisin breads, garlic,

and pierogies from the Polish vendor
who assures us,
he'll be here all winter.

Flamingo

We found it at a yard sale. For twenty years,
it stood in the battered wooden barrel

that was here when we bought our summer house.
It watched over us through winter snow.

This July, pink faded, body cracked, it toppled over.
We hauled it to the Easthampton dump

where it will mingle with the earth.
Scraped the barrel's dead leaves away,

added fertilizer, dug impatiens into the soil.
Every day we watered the flowers,

hovered over them like anxious parents
who thought their children would never leave them.

Limited Editions

Our neighbors, the Leibers, married 72 years,
died today in East Hampton, two hours apart,

ages 96 and 97. "It's time to go, Sweetie,"
Gerson, still painting, told Judith. When we drive

on Old Stone Highway, pass by their estate,
I think of her exquisite brocaded

handbag designs carried by Jackie Kennedy,
Princess Diana, Barbara Bush,

without straps in the shape of fans, eggs, pigs.
You could hardly fit anything into the tiny clutches—

a lipstick, a hundred-dollar bill.
Limited editions, as we are.

Pairs

On Verona Park's curved Japanese bridge,
a wedding couple pose for a photo;

the bride's train trails like a peacock's tail.
I sit in the sunshine, reading *Anna Karenina*.

She's moving out of Count Vronsky's house,
their bed of passion unmade.

You lean on your cane,
skip flat stones across the lake.

In the weeds, a pair of mallards
shake their feathers dry.

Anna waits on the railway platform
for the train. I want to rush

to the station, cry out, "Don't jump."
But I can't change the ending.

II

Our Buddha

At a farmstand,
we found the Buddha,
placed him in front
of our summer house.

I know little of his teachings,
but when I return from the beach
he looks at me
as if he knows who I am.

When night comes,
he sits outside
under the pale moon,
the distant stars.

Summer's end,
I bring him inside
to protect him
from cold and snow.

Already the red and gold
on his body
have faded a little.

Kugel

You have no appetite—
could be the meds.
Cranberry juice, flan, rice pudding—
"tastes terrible," you say.

The last time I baked a potato kugel
I was in my twenties,
recipe written in the blank back pages
of *From Abalone to Zabaglione,*
my first cookbook.

I measure out a cup of butter
and two of flour,
grate three small onions
and four potatoes by hand.
Add three eggs.

You take a forkful,
then push your plate away,
say, "I don't feel great,
I'll lie down for a bit."
I scrape your kugel onto my plate.

Caretaker

I fill your pillbox,
cut the one-half dosage evenly,
choose a vanilla Ensure
to help you swallow your meds.
It's time for dinner. I'm hungry;

you're not. I clear the table,
tell myself, "stop cooking."
But I love to sauté the onions,
toss in the broccoli, stir in the ginger soy.

I read Shoprite's specials,
not for the bargains but to see
the carrot cake, the scones.

You call out,
the pain is too much.
I give you two tramadol.
When you're asleep,

carry the trash to the curb,
stand in the driveway,
look up at the blank sky.

Crime Show

When you first got sick,
you sat in front of the TV
watching the same crime show,
volume turned up.
With my hearing aids in,
when I walked by, it sounded
like a war zone.
I couldn't get you to change the channel.
The murder taking place on the screen
drowned out the silence between us.
What was there to say?
You stayed there for hours,
looking straight ahead
as if you had already entered
another world.

Underworld

Going down the subway steps,
you hold the rail tightly,
panting a little as you descend.

Your legs go slowly, knees adjust.
You let others pass you
until the underworld takes over.

Down there, no wind,
no clouds, no sky, no ocean.
You swipe your MetroCard,

careful to hold it the right way.
People pass through turnstiles,
like Shades. You follow them

down the long dark tunnel,
those who gave up
their rights to the sun.

There are hundreds,
trying to live in a new world,
like you, where you will be immortal.

Two or three minutes until the beast
that will carry you
to your new connection comes.

End of the Line

You lie in the hospital bed,
eyes closed, waiting—
no hurry.

Got off at the last stop.
Stripped of everything,
you remember no one,

no place or thing.
Don't call.
Never make a sound.

You have no wrinkles, no fat.
I've started to wear
your Woonsocket

and U of Penn T-shirts.
It is the empty house,
the quiet, that kills.

Paradox

Your books huddle together
on shelves like abandoned lovers,
begging to be read aloud.

I count thirty-five by Irish authors.
Like Joyce you loved to quote:
"Do you think life is a paradox?"

A quiet man, you let yourself be
in *The Wake*'s lines without punctuation,
running each other over.

Oxygen mask removed,
breath stopped, pulse silent,
the attendants carried you away.

Not the way the hero goes out
in a forties movie, smile on his face.
"Here's lookin' at you, kid!"

The Men Die First

In ancient Hindu ceremony,
the widow threw herself on the pyre;
Victorian widows wore black veils.

We women cremate our men,
then a memorial ceremony.
Each in our own way mourns—

daughter, quiet; sister-in-law,
hysterical; me, distant.
We rearrange our lives.

The tumultuous tilt of loss.
The crossword puzzles
pile up on your desk.

Long Division

Bones burned to cinder,

you're without a body.

All the tangled sweetness

between us, disappeared.

Everything has or will be gone.

The earth, the graves.

Darkness, light.

The kisses like sugar in our mouths.

The longing.

The divided, the undivided.

Happiness, unhappiness.

This morning I found your razors

in the medicine chest.

Your Sensodyne toothpaste,

cap closed tight.

A Space

After boxing up the suits in your closet,
the ties hanging on the rack,
comes clearing out your desk.

After I find your master's diploma in the file
next to the house deed, after I touch
your father's gold cuff links,

read an essay you wrote in college on motivation,
I look up at the bookshelves—
five Thomas Pynchon novels,

a row of Isaac Bashevis Singer,
Groucho: The Life and Times.
After I throw away your worn wallet

with social security card, driver's license,
I find a newspaper clipping about a restaurant
in Woonsocket, Rhode Island,

the town you left behind but when mentioned,
always made you smile.
This thickening feeling,

like the empty lots of my childhood.
There is such a space
to cross to where you are.

They Have No Words

I find your ceramics
in cabinets, on shelves—

bowls, mugs, a teapot.
Line them up on the coffee table.

The ones you made
at North Carolina Pottery Center.

Those fired in Provincetown
where you bent over the wheel,

hoping to make your pots light.
I dust them, caress them,

feel your quiet. Who you were.
Day and night, your pottery stands there.

Some have cracks, others
have lost their bright glaze.

Leaves

Your ashes float like the white dust
of the blackboard erasers the teacher let
her favorite student clap.
Are you in the sky? As a girl,
I believed my parents were there.

On clear winter nights I found them
among the stars.
Silly child; silly woman;
the dead are dead and live nowhere.

In early October the leaves fall
from trees to earth and are carted away.
They feel no exquisite pain
as you did your last weeks, pulse failed,
no longer speaking or hearing.

The rattle of the red leaves
is a cry, a shout, to remember
your weekly visits to a museum,
driving our two granddaughters
to and from nursery school.
All that you were fallen away.

III

Dust

Cloudy October day, your mail to sort out,
leftovers in the fridge to toss.

It's hard to cook for just me.
I drink some coffee—

read the *Times* online—
take a quick look at the financial pages,

glance at the headlines.
Hatreds everywhere.

But I have my hands to write
away the emptiness

that lingers in the bedroom corners.
From everything, a little remains.

Saved postcards from the granddaughters at camp.
The jars of honey you loved.

Vanilla

Vanilla comes from orchids
that bloom beside graves.
In Spanish it means "little pod."
The Aztecs named it *tilxochitl*, "little flower."
It makes me feel like a little flower.
It is the second most expensive spice
after saffron. I don't care.
I brought back ten pods from Veracruz.
Their fragrance anoints me with sweetness.
I peel them open, sniff them,
get a little high,
drink from bottles of extract,
drown my throat.
Vanilla has no expiration date.

Joy

How they love death in Mexico.
I never knew there was such joy
in the dying of the body.

Tongue, nose, ears, gone.
Like a shrine, our living room shelf
holds a skeleton from Morelia.

Black dress, veil lacy white,
she holds a shriveled fan.
Rows of gray-black pots from Oaxaca

sit beside the ones you fired
until you couldn't anymore.
Chichén Itzá Mayans buried their dead

with maize in their mouths,
so they would have food for their journey.
You climbed to the pyramid's top.

O your teeth, O mouth throbbing.
O your body, breathless,
that used to burn.

Down Mexico Way

I hear Death on the rooftop, strumming a guitar,
singing, *South of the border, down Mexico way!*
          At the outdoor market, Death pretends
to be just another American tourist,

squeezing avocadoes for their ripeness.
He peeks at my Facebook page to see
          how many friends I have.
Not Death of the big black cloak

and scythe, but the one in the red jacket
and straw hat, the waiter at La Cocina
          taking my order for *pozole.*
You join me, light up a cigarillo,

order *huevos rancheros* and *Nestlé Abuelita.*
I tell you about the January 6 Hearings,
          give you the passcode for wi-fi,
so you can catch up.

You aren't interested, pay the bill
with cash, and vanish.
          The smiling waiter comes to the table,
asks, "How many for dinner? *Senora?*"

My One

I join the town pool,
senior hour, 10 to 11, stand chest deep

in the water until the young families burst in
like young princes and princesses.

I swim toward you, but you're apart from me,
have forgotten my name, what we talked about.

There are no words, only your dying
like a dried fig on a soft afternoon.

I tell myself it happens to everyone.
But you're my one.

Your death, a storm, a wasteland
I pass through, in love with the earth,

its skies, its oceans. A small wind starts up.
Your breath.

Progress Report

Boredom all day, television in the evening.
I pump my own gas, set the thermostat
for standard time, program the all-night lamp,
change the bills to automatic deduction,

Thursdays carry the everyday trash
to the curb—Wednesdays, comingled.
Will I ever learn which is which?
I am not falling, have an appetite,

barbeque on the new electric grill
with Mexican and Indian sauces
from Trader Joe's.
I found a denim shirt on sale

that snaps, no buttons to fight with.
My body doesn't creak.
I can walk up and down stairs.
My pink sweatshirt is warm and fits.

Whatever It Takes

I don't teach English Composition
at 8 am anymore.

Dream up topics for articles—
"The Blackbird's Wings in Wallace Stevens."

Rush to the supermarket
for a prepared salad and quiche.

Now I bake prune cake,
watch Netflix historical dramas—

the Bolshevik Revolution, Anne Boleyn.
Take naps, read the *Times* online.

So much to do—shove dirty clothes
into a pillowcase to throw down the steps.

How light it feels. I feel light too.
I do whatever it takes

to stay alive while I wait to join you
in an orbit of stars.

Letter to You

My love, you left your running shoes
on the closet rack.
Forgive me, I gave them away.
I am not suffering.
I lie, a little.
My hearing is getting worse.
I cling to the railing
when I walk downstairs.
I have a terrible fear
of falling down alone.
My front tooth fell out.
Yesterday I changed two lightbulbs
in the chandelier over our dining room table,
admiring the black finish
leafy-flowered decoration.
congratulated myself
on turning each bulb tight,
stood in the artificial brightness.
In the yard, squirrels chase each other.
Nothing can ruin being alive.

IV

Living Is All

You don't come to me in dreams.
Perhaps you've found another woman
in the sky where the polygamous gods live.

Here on earth at the feeder,
a hummingbird flaps its wings.
I have eggs for breakfast.

Find a book of world poetry
at the thrift shop. Only $5.00.
On the bay beach, shells under my feet,

I pick up a snail, brush it clean
with my fingers. It has no fragrance,
didn't live long.

I tossed your ashes into this bay,
to think of you when I walk here.
And all the while there is delight.

Be Happy

Evening gathers in a long-stemmed goblet.
The night lamp turns on, guiding me.

Steam rises from the teakettle,
a car starts up—a neighbor going to the 7-Eleven.

Outside, from two trees, the hammock sags
like an old woman. *Be happy,*

commands the song on my iPad.
Boil pasta, load the dishwasher,

pour grief into a wineglass.
Remind myself of the beautiful children

in strollers I stop to ogle. The yellow forsythia,
the peonies deep red, suddenly here.

On Parole

I take my walk in the park,
past the bocce court,
the fenced-off playground.

Children swing, mothers push.
A lone cherry tree is pink
as the L.L. Bean kerchief I wear.

Alone, my heart stained
with regret,
you are a wrinkled shadow.

It would be marvelous to run
around the lake,
shouting, "I'm still here!"

To stand
on the bridge waving
hello.

This Happiness

To be in the kitchen,
darkness falling at 4:46 pm,
backyard hill fading
into the landscape,
deer no longer
climbing down,
these apparitions,
haunting the suburbs.

On WQXR, Haydn,
and me dancing little steps,
thinking lucky, O lucky,
as I count my years
on my fingers.
I haven't left my house
for days, waiting for the sun
like a refilled prescription.

Who said, "Old age
ain't for sissies?"
My brother, an aficionado
of forties movies,
said it was Bette Davis.

And yet, this happiness
in my kitchen, slicing
an acorn squash,
squeezing lemon
on the flounder.
Just me.

Three-Day Weekend

Monday, a national holiday,
everyone is at the shore.

I take refuge in what is alive—
the small landscape of the hill.

The earth rolling down it.
Beethoven vibrates on my cell phone.

Dinner is on the deck at the patio table
covered with a new flowered cloth.

It has a zipper and an umbrella hole.
Hours on Amazon to find it.

I carry your push broom from the garage.
Its stiff bristles come apart.

The trash men will cart my sweepings
to the dump where dead things go.

I, a root, search for a tree
to attach myself to.

Spring Again

June has come, lightly.
Paddleboats ply the lake.
Kids scream and laugh.
Couples sit on benches,
nod and smile as I pass.

A man walks toward me,
His face a lamp lit up
by morning sun.
He's not bent over,
doesn't carry a cane.

I can't remember what stupid thing
I said to start the conversation.
I told him my name.
He said it was his wife's,
gone three years now.

Roses are blossoming
on this marvelous spring day.
He takes out his flip phone,
asks for my number.
I haven't lost the art of flirting.

Lines Written at Louse Point

This June afternoon cool and clear,
home between school end and summer camp,
kids run along the pebbled bay.

Someone's small dog nuzzles me.
On the bay path, beach plums redden.
Gusts of wind, nostalgia—

the salt smell of time past, the Jersey shore,
circled beach chairs, aunts and uncles
gossiping. Buried by my brother,

up to my neck in sand. Each summer
I migrate to this point and watch
the green islands ringed in brown

rise from the bay's bottom,
paddle out to them, dipping the oars
deep in water until the canoe scrapes

shallow shoals near beached fish,
white bellies up. One stroke,
then another, reach land.

Along the shoreline, a flock of terns
skitter as they rise. Sun flickers
like a faulty showerhead.

The past wears away until nothing is left.
I am nearly finished
with the wind and the wild grasses.

Still Me

My body is becoming an empty room.
June fills the night.
In the backyard, rhododendron bloom.
Kids build a sand castle like a tomb.

I did the dead man's float in the sea.
Beyond the horizon bombed-out cities loom.
June fills the night; soon I'll no longer be.
I brew, then pour chamomile tea,

a woman who faces this world's doom
without belief in eternity.
My body is becoming an empty room.
T. S. Eliot, his métier doom,

wrote "human kind cannot bear very much reality."
I make up my face, spray on perfume.
It took years to write about me.
Once more the world's gone crazy.

It does no good to fume.
Death will find me inevitably.
In the backyard, rhododendron bloom.
Sun sinks into my beloved sea.

Overhead a full moon will loom.
I am here, still me.
I listen to the Atlantic breakers boom.
June fills the night.

V

Egg

It's down to you,
soft-boiled egg
in a tiny ceramic cup,
spoon tapping your shell,
the way the English do.
Yolk yellow as the sun,
you are victory over decay.
I salt you,
spoon your goodness up,
enter your poet's soul.
You who are more than taste,
real as the life I've lived,
you exist
in my mouth
like a lover's tongue,
remind me I am alive.
Dear egg, forgive me
for not believing
in an afterlife.
You are enough.

Return Visit

You enter our front door,
eyes glued to your cell phone.
Perhaps you are buying stuff on Amazon.
What could you possibly need?

Maybe you called customer service
and are on hold. Or making
airline reservations not caring
if our flight is cancelled,

having already reached your destination.
You linger in the kitchen,
eye the spinach lasagna
made for New Year's Eve.

Forgetting the dead don't eat or drink,
I offer you a glass of your favorite
Mexican drink, *horchata*.
We whirl to Latin rock.

Like a flamenco dancer,
arms raised, I clap my hands,
close my eyes. When I open them,
you are gone again.

Gift

When my end comes,
I will become a dusty cloud,
looking down on the shameful earth.
See ruined cities
whose names I can't pronounce.

On the day they carry me off,
my mouth closed tight
like the shirt my fingers
can no longer button,
will I shake with terror?

No longer moved by the sun's light
in air and sky.
Never again to see gulls
glide through space.

The first blizzard of the year arrives
like the first snow of my life
when my eyes opened in amazement.
A grown-up's hands
lifted me to the window to watch
this glittering gift—
delicate flakes, sparkling.

A Day Behind

Spring sun with all its braggadocio
signals I exist. The light of April,
my birth month, comes through the window.

I run to the park in tie-dye clogs.
Canada geese have gathered.
End of day, bedroom TV.

I note the year each film was made.
Mysteries—the detective
and his sidekick, a man and a woman,

attracted to each other, never sleep together.
A rainstorm is predicted.
I'm always a day behind the calendar.

A Question of Travel

Travel brochures come in the mail.
Today, a trip to Petra, Jordan,

its requirement: to climb Al-Khazneh Temple,
45 feet high, you must be fit.

I drop it into the basket
with weeks of the *Times*.

Read supermarket holiday offers:
hams, turkeys, Easter bunnies, matzo.

Order an English shepherd's pie
to help me stop the longing.

Tell myself: look around you, Carole.
See how the forsythia spring up yellow.

Birth, birth, it can't be stopped.
Even the rain smells of life.

The Lost

I have travelled long with the lost.
They didn't expect to leave, couldn't say good-bye,

lingered, wanting one more meal,
one more drink, a final kiss.

The silence of their mouths like knives,
they were lifted up into the dust of the sky.

Their bodies stretched far out,
they look down at the tiny earth.

In the everyday, corned beef simmers four hours.
The neighbor's chimes ring in the wind.

Evenings, full of those who are gone,
I leave the porchlight on.

Spine

The carp gasps for air,
while I sink the Chinese chopping knife

into its silvery scales, steam it in ginger,
lay the fish on a blue porcelain platter,

honor it with lemon roses as the ancients did.
At last, I have the patience

to lift the flesh from the bony spine,
learn to hold chopsticks,

raising each morsel to my lips.
Li-Po, drunkenly reaching for the moon

in a pond, fell in. Whatever is to come
I am glad I've picked these bones bare.

On That Day

I will die in New Jersey on a cool day.
It will be early September.

A Monday because today is Monday.
The kids will have gone back to school.

My poetry books will join your novels.
I will find endings for the poems stored

in my files like the yellow pages
no one reads. Give away

the pantsuits I wore for teaching.
Join you in your faded army fatigues.

Tell you, "it wasn't so bad,
our lives together."

We will lie down, the two of us,
almost strangers.

ACKNOWLEDGMENTS

The published poems in this manuscript have appeared in the following journals:

Adanna: "In the Matter of Pumpkin Soup," "Pairs"
Crossroads: "Spine"
Journal of New Jersey Poets: "This Happiness"
Last Leaves: "One by One"
Pen and Brush: "Egg"
The Pine Cone Review: "Letter to You," titled "Letter to My
   Husband"
Sequestrum: "Long Marriage"
Slab: "Day Trip to Brighton"
Verse-Virtual: "Paradox," "Progress Report," "A Space,"
   "Underworld"

The poem "Flamingo" was published in the anthology
Meta-Land, Poets of the Palisades II, edited by Paul Nash,
Denise La Neve, David Messineo, Susanna Rich, and John J.
Trause (Pittsburgh, Pennsylvania: The Poet's Press, 2016).

The poem "Spine" was first published in the chapbook *More
Sweet, More Salt* (Georgetown, Kentucky: Finishing Line
Press, 2005).

Thanks to the many poets, too numerous to name, from
East Hampton, New York to New Jersey for their invaluable
critiques of my poems. A special thanks to Susanna Rich for
her thoughtful readings of my work.

CAVANKERRY'S MISSION

A not-for-profit literary press serving art and community, CavanKerry is committed to expanding the reach of poetry and other fine literature to a general readership by publishing works that explore the emotional and psychological landscapes of everyday life, and to bringing that art to the underserved where they live, work, and receive services.

OTHER BOOKS IN THE NOTABLE VOICES SERIES

Deep Are These Distances Between Us, Susan Atefat-Peckham
The History Hotel, Baron Wormser
Dialect of Distant Harbors, Dipika Mukherjee
The Snow's Wife, Frannie Lindsay
Eleanor, Gray Jacobik
Without My Asking, Robert Cording
Miss August, Nin Andrews
A Car Stops and a Door Opens, Christopher Bursk
Letters from Limbo, Jeanne Marie Beaumont
Tornadoesque, Donald Platt
Only So Far, Robert Cording
Unidentified Sighing Objects, Baron Wormser
How They Fell, Annie Boutelle
The Bar of the Flattened Heart, David Keller
Same Old Story, Dawn Potter
The Laundress Catches Her Breath, Paola Corso
American Rhapsody, Carole Stone
Impenitent Notes, Baron Wormser
Walking with Ruskin, Robert Cording
Divina Is Divina, Jack Wiler
How the Crimes Happened, Dawn Potter
Descent, John Haines
Southern Comfort, Nin Andrews
Losing Season, Jack Ridl

Limited Editions was typeset in Arno Pro, which was created by Robert Slimbach at Adobe. The name refers to the river that runs through Florence, Italy.